THE
SANDPLAY CATEGORICAL CHECKLIST
FOR
SANDPLAY ANALYSIS

THE SANDPLAY CATEGORICAL CHECKLIST

for

SANDPLAY ANALYSIS

Geri Grubbs, Ph.D.

Rubedo Publications

17512 185th Ave. NE, Woodinville, WA 98072

Rubedo Publishing
17512 185th Ave. NE, Woodinville, Washington 98072.

First printed in 1997 by Geri Grubbs as
"The Sandtray Categorical Checklist for Sandtray Assessment."

ISBN 0-9765431-0-9

ATTENTION ORGANIZATIONS, PSYCHOTHERAPY CENTERS, AND SCHOOLS OF SPIRITUAL DEVELOPMENT:
Quantity discounts are available on bulk purchases of this manual for educational purposes or fund raising. Special booklets or book excerpts can also be created to fit specific needs. For information, please contact

Rubedo Publishing
17512 185th Ave. NE, Woodinville, WA 98072,
or
Geri Grubbs at www.EastsideJung.com.

This manual is dedicated to the

devoted children who participated weekly

in my research

Also by Geri Grubbs

"Bereavement Dreaming and the Individuating Soul"

Nicolas-Hays, Inc., Berwick, ME 03901

TABLE OF CONTENTS

Part I: Introduction

Part II: Category Descriptions

Direct Observations and Objective Analysis

Subjective Impressions and Implied Meanings

PART I

INTRODUCTION

Purpose

The SCC is a sandplay assessment tool composed of qualitative, descriptive categories that amplify specific aspects of sandplay construction. It contains a detailed listing of all known modes of expression in the making of a sandtray with a focus on patterns of change from one tray to the next.

The checklist was originally constructed for the purpose of analyzing and comparing the sandplay process of abused and nonabused children[1]. Guidelines in its construction follow Ruth Bowyer's research on developmental norms[2], L. Jones' cognitive-developmental studies[3], Jeannette Reed's research on children with learning disabilities[4] and the theories formulated by Carl Jung and Dora Kalff[5]. This unique checklist is especially useful for beginning sandplay therapists seeking guidlines for sandplay analysis, for advanced therapists desiring an in-depth and thorough study of a specific sandplay process, and for research in sandplay therapy.

Structure and Use of the SCC

The SCC is composed of 19 categories that utilize three aspects of sandplay construction: (1) the thematic content of the tray and the process involved in creating it, (2) the creator's personal report or story of what the tray signifies to them, and (3) the progressive or regressive changes that occur from one tray to the next. It is divided into two main sections according to the type of analysis made. The first section, "direct observation and objective analysis," contains objective/quantitative listings (i.e., figures used, setting, animals used as people). These categories are clear-cut and obvious with little subjective interpretation made by the therapist. The second section, "subjective impressions and implied meanings," is composed of inferential/interpretive listings (i.e., self-nurturing expressive play, no coordination of scene). These categories call for the therapist's subjective interpretation and require some sandplay experience and knowledge of human development. In certain situations and especially in research, it is significant as to whether or not, and how much of, the therapist's subjective impressions are involved in the final analysis.

The master SCC may be found on page 21. Copy as many as you need for each sandtray created. You may fill out the checklist as your client creates the tray in recording the story, figures used, and the dramatic play. It is important to be as non-intrusive as possible while your client works and to put his/her needs before the checklist, which can always be returned to later. After your client leaves, other categories can be checked quickly as you sit in front of the tray, or you may complete it later when studying the photo you have taken. It is best to complete the SCC as soon as possible after the tray is made so that you can recall its many details.

Taking a Polaroid or digital picture of all sandtrays is necessary if you want to follow the sequence of scenes in a process that can easily span months or even years. If you do not have access to a camera, then you should at least

draw a diagram of the scene. In this case, it would be best to fill out the checklist prior to dismantling the tray, or its many details may be lost. The picture or diagram can then be attached to the SCC. In addition to taking a photo for the client's file, many sandtray therapists routinely take slide or digital pictures of the whole and parts of the tray to use in following their client's detailed process, in reviewing a sandtray process with their client long after the last tray is made, and for educational purposes.

One may easily use a series of checklists of their client's process to assess changes and regressions or progressions from one tray to the next within a specific category. This is done by compiling the recordings in each category in sequence. As an example: Category 3 - Setting: Tray 1- disorganized and primitive; Tray 2 - disorganized; Tray 3 - war; Tray 4 - community and war; Tray 5 - celebration; Tray 6 - Oriental; Tray 7 - Self tray; Tray 8 - animal/ vegetative; Tray 9 - community; Tray 10 - symbolic. From this, progressive changes in one category can be clearly seen.

The SCC is not intended to be used to interpret sandtrays to a client while he/she is seeing you. It is an assessment tool for the therapist only. Saying to clients that they are regressing, showing disturbances in what they've created, or even expressing the core part of the Self can interfere with the growth and resolution process that may come into being. The beginning sandplay therapist should read at least one or several of the many books that have been written about sandtray or sandplay therapy. In the following category descriptions, meanings are given for various portrayals based upon previous research; however this only skims the surface of sandplay assessment. Several very good books are listed in the bibliography and resource section at the end of this manual that may further help you with a possible meaning behind certain portrayals. If you are in the learning process, you are encouraged to use these books along with the SCC.

PART II

CATEGORY DESCRIPTIONS

Direct Observation and Objective Analysis

1. Story

During or after the making of a sandtray, individuals may describe what they see happening in the scene or what the figures and particulars mean to them. Often this is done on their own or may be asked for in a non-intrusive way by the therapist. These descriptions and direct quotes add the very important perspective of the creator to the process and are an important aspect of sandplay therapy. If the creator prefers to make the sandtray in silence and not talk about it (it is important not to intrude on this), then "no story" is written in the space provided.

2. Figures (and meanings if verbalized)

Most quantitative, this category is primarily a naming and numbering of figures in the tray (i.e.: animals, people, structures, objects, vehicles, natural

elements, etc.). It is not intended to be a counting of figures; but rather, a recording of items and their meanings when voluntarily verbalized by the creator. However, in certain situations, numbers may have symbolic significance (i.e., when a particular number of bridges are used in several trays, or when a specific number of groupings are repeated in various parts of the same tray). The significance associated with these numbers can be found in various symbol dictionaries, some of which are noted in the bibliography.

3. Setting

The combination of theme and environment constitutes the setting and is an aspect of the world view of the creator. Worlds may be disorganized with no apparent theme, family oriented, symbolic, spiritual, and so forth. The first part of this category lists the many different kinds of settings that are often created. Disorganized settings have no coherent theme to them, primitive settings contain many cold-blooded creatures such as dinosaurs, snakes and crocodiles, and bizarre settings have an alien, satanic-like quality to them. Wound trays are an expression of a deep wounding to the psyche and appear as painful eruptions of primitive and enraged emotions. Self trays are mandala, square or spherical-shaped designs in the center of the tray that radiate a spiritual quality, and are indicative of the Self or soul expression of the creator. The list of settings come from the research of Bowyer and Kalff and Grubbs' research on sexually abused children.

The second part of this category focuses on the orientation of the setting which is either content or theme, or a combination of both. Some people use figures or symbols to represent specific aspects of their outer or inner life in a more static way (content), while others create stories in which there is movement and relationship between the figures (theme). Bowyer found that as children mature, they tend to create worlds that are more theme than content oriented. The followers of Kalff have observed that when portrayals come from the depths of the psyche, they tend to be more content oriented. Both are

significant in assessing the individual's cognitive development (Bowyer) and progress within the sandplay process (Kalff).

4. Creation process/Dramatic play

This category focuses on the movement or dramatic action that transpires in the creation process. Individuals vary in the way they create their tray, some positioning figures in one spot, others moving figures around or playing dramatically the entire time. Dramatic play is common with young children; whereas, adults tend to make picture-like trays. Bowyer believed that the use of action is a good prognostic sign for a child. This category is important in analyzing developmental norms as well as the creator's expressive mode and dramatic interactions with self and others.

The list of items in this category includes the various changes or non-changes in sandplay creation. When major changes are made during the making of the tray or when dramatic play is part of the creation, you may record the specifics in the space provided. With young children, action and change may be constant, requiring a separate page to record all that appears significant in the play process.

5. Use of human and animal figures

The use of human and animal figures and how they are portrayed within the setting is the focus of this category. In the research of both Bowyer and Grubbs, it was observed that a child's use or non-use of human and animal figures relates significantly to family conflicts, emotional disturbances and physical health. (See Guidelines for Sandplay Analysis in Appendix A).

Included in this category are three separate columns and a fill in: the first column lists the various ways figures are used. The second and third are symptomatic portrayals and representations. If the creator uses an observer, an obvious figure watching the action in the scene, this should be recorded in the space provided. It is believed that such a figure is a representation of the conscious observing ego of the individual making the tray.

6. Use of sand

The first part of this category records the creator's choice of dry or wet sand.

The second part contains a listing of ways the creator uses or does not use the sand in creating their world scene. Previous research (Bowyer, Grubbs, Jones) has shown that there is a vast difference in how people use or engage with the sand. Some clearly avoid touching the sand, some use it to fully structure their worlds, and others may use the sand to bury figures and destroy their creations. Bowyer considered an individual's willingness to mold and structure their sand world as a sophisticated sign which normally does not become evident before the age of eleven. She believes that those who mold the sand are able to use their inner, creative resources in adapting to their environment. Some sandplay therapists believe that an individual's unwillingness to touch the sand suggests a disconnection from the mother-element or center of the self.

Write-in space is provided for items that are buried. When figures or objects are buried, it suggests a repression or disconnection from what the item represents. This is especially the case when done by adults. However, it is developmentally normal for children under the age of five to bury objects and poke them into the sand.

The "Use of Sand" category contains the many different ways one can

interact with the sand, including use of water to wet and mold it. At times, water may be used to completely flood the tray, suggesting an emotional discharge and the possible expression of trauma (Grubbs). Very young children up to about age four will naturally flood their worlds, which is generally considered a part of their developmental play.

7. Use of tray

Some individuals fill the sandtray with figures and objects to its fullest capacity while others place only one or two objects in it. The end product can result in a world that looks overflowing, another full and complete, while yet another may appear quite empty. In her research, Bowyer found that nonclinical children create scenes in which they use most, if not all, areas of the tray. She also found that very young nonclinical children could easily fill a tray to its fullest capacity with objects spilling over the sides and onto the floor.

In her case studies, Kalff observed that there are moments in the sandplay process when a mandala or square is made in the center of the tray. Both Kalff and Jung view this as a manifestation or image of the Self that comes forth from a tension of opposites that evolve from the creative process. Such Self and archetypal expressions arise directly from the collective unconscious, revealing in its unique way the archetypes that are actively involved in the healing process. Often the making of a Self tray can lead to a slightly changed attitude in one's everyday world. These trays may appear empty with no human figures, yet project a beauty and radiance that goes beyond words. It is not unusual for the creator to experience feelings of transcendence upon observing what he/she has made. Yasunobu Okada observed that even in creations of an everyday reality, clients may add objects to the center space of the tray that are suggestive of their inner Self or collective unconscious. Because of the tendency of this space to hold a numinous aura, he refers to it as the "Self space." [6]

The "Use of Tray" category contains a main list running across the page and three separate items for fill-in. The main list itemizes specific ways that sandtrays are used. The three fill-in items include:

1) the main focal areas of the tray - areas that contain the major action or energy;

2) large areas of empty space;

3) figures that are placed in the center of the tray or the "Self space."

8. Creator's response

As worlds are made or when completed, the creator may experience strong feelings or repressed memories may be brought to consciousness. Bowyer found that some children express highly aggressive emotions as they play in the sand, indicating a positive working-through of their feelings. Adults, too, may express angry emotions as they create their scenes or cry as they sit and observe what they've made. It is best to record the creator's response immediately following the completion of the sandtray, during the picture-taking process. Emotions may have been openly verbalized by the creator or they may have been sensed by the therapist, giving the data recorded a more subjective interpretation.

Subjective Impressions and Implied Meanings

9. Main psychological expressions

Every sandtray contains a psychological expression that is closely intertwined with the story, setting and emotions (i.e., destruction, competition, self-protection, celebration, uniting of opposites, etc.). The first part of this

category contains a list of fourteen expressions, with write-in space provided if the expression that you have observed is not included. More than one expression in a scene may occur.

These expressions may be portrayed as realistic enactments of everyday life, as fantasy, or a combination of both. The second part of this category contains a 5-point Likert scale between reality and fantasy, where the degree of both is recorded with a checkmark. For example: if the scene is a true portrayal of one's home, this would be a fully realistic scene; whereas if a home contains a mythical or symbolic character, the scene would be part reality and part fantasy. Worlds high in fantasy come from that part of the psyche that Jung refers to as the collective unconscious. [7]

10. Cognitive development and scene progress

This category includes two separate, yet related, aspects of sandplay: the chronological age appearance of the creation and progressions or regressions in the sandplay process itself. In the "Cognition" aspect, the apparent chronological age of the sand creation is recorded. This may be the same, or regressive/progressive to the chronological age of the creator. (Turn to Developmental Norms under Guidelines for Sandtray Analysis in Appendix A as an aid in making this assessment.)

According to the cognitive-developmental theory of Jean Piaget,[8] and as observed in the research of Bowyer and Jones, if an individual creates a scene that appears to be immature, a developmentally regressive delay may be a part of his/her approach toward life. This is especially so if the regressive portrayal is expressed in a continuous series of sandtrays. If expressed once or twice, the regression may be a temporary relapse prior to a new level of psychological change. More about this dynamic expression will be presented in the next category, Coordination of Whole and Parts of the Scene.

In the second column of "Cognitive Development and Scene Progress, progressions or regressions in the sandplay process are recorded. A previous sandtray is necessary for this comparison to be made. The sandtray may be continuous with little change from the previous tray, regressive in development or content, progressive in development or content, or progressive in that an earlier scene is clearly restructured. This assessment is somewhat of a judgment call on the part of the therapist, so it helps to have some experience with sandplay therapy to make an adequate assessment. Restructuring of a scene is apparent when one tray contains the same theme and figures as a previously-made tray, but with a slightly different arrangement or connecting link. Such trays may indicate that a resolution of conflict or a uniting of opposites has taken place.

11. Coordination of whole and parts of the scene

The organization or lack of organization within parts of the tray or the tray as a whole is an important aspect of sandtray creation. Based on her research, Bowyer suggested that a continuous lack of organization in a series of sandtrays after the age of twelve may indicate an emotional or intellectual conflict, or a regressive approach toward life. Bowyer also observed that a disorganization in one or two trays sometimes occurs when this was not the pattern in previous trays. She viewed this temporary disorganization as a working through of earlier developmental issues prior to a new level of psychological growth. Kalff observed in her case studies that there often is an intrinsic ordering or coming together of parts or the whole of the scene as individuals work in the sand over a period. Often this intrinsic ordering evolves into the creation of a Self tray, an expression of the true Self of the individual. As presented earlier, this is considered a healing portrayal in sandplay.

The first list in the category contains the various degrees of scene coordination, from chaotic to fully coordinated. Selecting what fits is a judgment call by the therapist. It helps to have experience in analyzing

sandtrays before an adequate assessment of this can be made. The second list contains factors in world creation that may indicate the presence of an emotional conflict or disturbance based on Bowyer's research.

12. Structuring of relationships (human and animal)

The focus of this category is on aspects of interpersonal organization and the interactions between them as researched by Jones. The first list of seven items contains dependence or interdependence of the figures with individual, dyadic, family and community structures. The second part contains the type of interactions portrayed, including destructive interactions indicative of conflicts in relationships, and cooperative, healthy interactions. This category is important in assessing the individual's view of humanity and feelings about self in relation to others.

13. Boundaries

The sandtray and what's created in it include boundaries on three dimensions: the external boundary of the tray, internal boundaries created within the scene, and the sand or base upon which the figures are placed (Bowyer, Jones). The creation or non-creation of external (tray) and base (sand) boundaries reflect the emotional and cognitive development of the subject. Mature individuals relate to the world with well-defined psychological boundaries and create these boundaries in their scene or on the sand. However, it is not unusual for an adult to set a figure or two on the edge of the tray. This should be assessed as part of the internal scene. Children younger than four years who naturally have undeveloped psychological boundaries create worlds that spill over the sides of the tray and don't hesitate to push figures down into the sand. Such expressions are considered normal for their age.

Internal boundaries within the individual's creation reflect their willingness to let others into their space or their need for protection or

separation from others (Bowyer, Jones). Rigid boundaries include fencing without entryways and heavy, solid sandwalls. Open boundaries contain gateways, connecting bridges, and roads from one area of the tray to another.

The first section lists whether or not boundaries are made and when made, the kind of boundary formed. The second section includes four kinds of dysfunctional boundaries that are occasionally created (Bowyer, Grubbs).

14. Movement/Obstacles

Movement within a world and the blockage of movement by obstacles or boundaries are related and important aspects of sandplay analysis. These are created in many ways. Through sand molding, rivers and roads connect, whereas sandwalls and mountains block. Natural elements, such as rocks and forests can either create movement or block it. Man-made elements such as a road blocked by a pile of cars obstruct movement, while two separate groups of people cooperating together express a dynamic interaction.

The portrayal of movement in ones world suggests an ability to grow and extend; whereas, blockages imply isolation and regressive trends in development. Both functional and dysfunctional styles of movements are listed in this category, and include partial blockages, destructive movement, and positive movement toward the center of the self.

15. Relationship of parts and opposites

Jung states that transformation involves a confrontation and uniting of opposites, which represents a transition from an old attitude or behavior to a new one. In sandplay therapy, such a relationship is portrayed through the uniting of different or significant areas of the tray, warring factions, masculine

and feminine figures, and so forth. The sand may be used to form roads or rivers that unite, man-made objects such as bridges may be used to connect two previously separated sides of the scene, and figures may be placed so that one observes or interacts with another of an opposite nature.[9]

There are two parts to this category. The first is a write-in space for significant opposites that appear to be portrayed in the scene. Opposites may or may not be represented and can be checked as such. The second part is a list of different interactions between these opposites and attempts to unify them if portrayed. Opposites may be already united (in relationship) or well integrated. The degree of unification is definitely a subjective interpretation. As in other categories, analysis of parts and opposites requires some experience in sandplay analysis and a basic knowledge of Jungian psychology.

16. Therapist's Impression

In this category, you record the feelings or impressions that you might have had while your client created the tray or what you feel as you look at the finished product. Your private impression provides further information about the emotional content of the scene, as observed from your witnessing self.

17. Significant symbolic representations and thematic play

In creative expression, healing occurs through the use and interaction of the symbol or archetypal image. In sandplay therapy, the use of the symbol may guide the psyche toward a resolution of unresolved conflicts and lead one toward new facets of one's deeper being. The therapist's knowledge of the meaning behind these symbols, significant figures and their movement, is a necessary adjunct to sandplay analysis. Kalff affirmed strongly that it is through the therapist's attention to the symbol and knowledge of its meaning in their

client's process that a deep understanding and connection to their healing is made.

This category provides a space for the recording of outstanding or unusual representations, such as circular formations that may lead to the eventual expression of the Self, the repetitive use or burying of a significant figure, and their possible meanings in the individual's process.

18. Significant repetitive theme and figures used

Similar to the previous category, this space is provided for the descriptive recording of symbolically relevant figures and themes that are used repetitively from one scene to the next.

19. Questions raised

What thoughts come to mind as you review the sandtray? Are you suspecting that a regression or progression may be taking place? Do you wonder about a particular figure that may be prominent in the process? This space is provided for whatever questions you may have as you observe, study and analyze this unique sandtray and the process as a whole.

APPENDIX A

GUIDELINES FOR SANDPLAY ANALYSIS

Developmental Norms

Ages 2-4   Use of only portions of the tray (edges, corners, etc.)
Sand used in pouring or burying
Figures poked or flung into the sand
Figures left buried or half buried
Worlds very chaotic and disordered
Heavy use of animal figures rather than people
Spilling of figures over the sides of the tray
Extreme similarity of world expression from one child to the next

Ages 5-7   Increased use of tray space
Small islands of order starting at age 4
Continues with heavy use of animal figures
Beginning of fenced or rigid worlds
Beginning of the fighting stage at age 7 (continuous battles
        between warring groups of soldiers, cowboys and Indians,
        knights, etc., especially with boys)
A great deal of dramatic activity and active play
Pouring sand over people and other figures
Eating topics often represented (how to feed the animals, etc.)

Ages 8-10   Fenced or rigid worlds peak at age 10 - formation of boundaries
Fighting stage continues
More emphasis on factual reality
As age increases, a more constructive use of sand develops (hills,
        roads, tunnels)
A gradual development toward a theme orientation

Ages 11+   World is gestalt oriented where the whole of the scene pulls
together
Organization of patterns and interdependence of parts is portrayed
Conceptual or symbolic representation of towns or villages
Landscapes with human settlements are common
From 11 to adolescence, jungle animals appear again, similar to
pre-school age, but now represented more realistically

Indications of Disturbance After Age Five

1. Very empty, lonely-appearing worlds - suggests withdrawal, apathy,
    inaccessibility.

2. Large portions of the tray ignored, except in specific situations with a highly
    symbolic quality. Some sparseness is okay when the spatial arrangement
    appears to be balanced.

3. Animals devouring other animals or people, except in realistic situations,
    such as an animal hunting its food.

4. Very disorganized worlds may indicate a regression to as far back as 2-4
    years of age.

5. Heavily fenced worlds with no gates or entryways - suggests a fear of
    impulses, a need to protect the inner Self, obsessional traits.

6. An overemphasis on having things in rows that have no justification in
    reality.

7. Burying of objects, pushing figures down into the sand, pouring sand over
    people and things - shows a regression and possible sadistic attitude
    toward oneself and others.

8. No human figure/s in the scene (unpeopled worlds) - suggests a feeling of
    alienation, fear of threat, etc., unless the scene is on an archetypal level.

9. Continuous sadistic violence on family members and vulnerable victims - suggests past trauma, abuse in the home, and/or self-abusive behavior.

10. An avoidance of or continuous failure to touch the sand - suggests a disconnection from the core part of the self.

11. Depiction of bizarre (satanic) and extremely primitive scenes (reptilian) - suggests a tendency toward psychosis.

12. Penning or crowding of figures into a tight mass - suggests an anal-sadistic attitude.

Indications of Strength, Progress, Working Through, Integration

1. A constructive use of sand through the molding of hills, valleys, rivers, tunnels - indicates a good use of creative resources in adapting to outer reality. Generally does not occur under age seven unless child has experience in sandplay.

2. The depiction of conflict in the outer or inner world with a gradual working through of this conflict.

3. Expression of aggression to resolve pent-up feelings.

4. A change from chaos to more order and especially a restructuring of previous scenes.

5. Brief regression, working through, and return to present level of development (usually depicted in several trays over a period) - shows the struggle to reorganize.

6. A growth in imagination and ingenuity.

7. More complex verbal descriptions of the happenings in the tray.

8. A uniting of opposites such as good/bad, far/near, left/right, portrayed with bridges, roads, rivers, etc. and/or dramatic play.

9. Progress in arrangement, logical patterns, and designs.

10. Highly symbolic or mythical representations portraying an inner, spiritual quality.

11. An internal ordering toward the center of the tray, often portrayed as a circle. Has a spiritual quality. Referred to by Kalff as a Self   tray that leads to a new level of development.

Guidelines are from the research of:

Ruth Bowyer, *The Lowenfeld world technique* (London: Pergammon Press, 1970).

Geri Grubbs, *A categorical and comparative analysis of the sand play process of abused and nonabused children.* Unpublished doctoral dissertation: California Graduate School of Family Psychology, San Rafael, CA, 1991.

Dora Kalff, *Sandplay: A psychotherapeutic approach to the psyche* (Santa Monica, California: Sigo Press, 1980).

APPENDIX B

THE SANDPLAY CATEGORICAL CHECKLIST
(SCC)

SANDPLAY CATEGORICAL CHECKLIST (SCC)

CREATOR:_____DATE:_____TRAY #:_____of_____

DIRECT OBSERVATION AND OBJECTIVE ANALYSIS

1. STORY (briefly worded)

_____
_____
_____
_____
_____
_____

2. FIGURES (and meanings if verbalized)

Animals:

_____
_____
_____

People:

_____
_____
_____

Structures (buildings, barriers, connectors, etc.):

_____
_____

Objects (furniture, jewelry, weapons, food, etc.):

_____
_____
_____

Vehicles:

_____
_____

Natural Elements and Vegetation:

_____
_____

Other:

_____
_____

3. SETTING

__disorganized	__animal/vegetative	__war	__Asian
__primitive	__people/animal	__community/city/village	__symbolic/mythical
__bizarre (explain)	__home/family	__party/celebration	__spiritual/Self tray
__wound tray			

_____.

Oriented as: ___Content   ___Theme

4. CREATION PROCESS/DRAMATIC PLAY

___scene made intact with few changes   ___dramatic play as scene is made (describe)

___major changes as scene is made (describe)   ___ scene made first - then change of any kind or resolution

___scene made - then destroyed (describe how)

_____

_____

5. USE OF HUMAN AND ANIMAL FIGURES

___used appropriately	___no human or animal figures used	___people killing people
___used realistically	___animals in place of people	___penned or crowded into a tight mass
___used symbolically	___broken and/or dismembered body parts	___buried or hidden from others
___implied but not used	___animals devouring animals/people	___placed in dangerous/precarious places
		___ intentionally knocked down and left

Observer (if used): _____

6. USE OF SAND

____Damp   ____Dry

___figures placed on top, sand untouched   ___intentionally thrown and splashed

___sand firmly packed down   ___used destructively by pouring and/or burying

___some movement of sand with finger tips   ___heavily wetted down

___diligently molded and shaped   ___half to whole of tray flooded

___sand used to bury_____

7. USE OF TRAY

___very empty   ___sparse   ___well used   ___full   ___very full   ___overflowing   ___2 trays together

Areas of focus_____

Empty areas_____

Figures placed in center_____

8. CREATOR'S RESPONSE TO SCENE

___indifferent or no response	___apologetic	___relieved	___deeply moved
___pushes it away	___emotional (sad, angry, excited)	___energized	
___sadistic toward it	___satisfied (somewhat / very)	___trancelike	

SUBJECTIVE IMPRESSIONS AND IMPLIED MEANINGS

9. MAIN PSYCHOLOGICAL EXPRESSIONS:

___destruction/violence   ___alienation/loneliness   ___organizing/structuring   ___worship

___aggression   ___self-protection   ___construction/building   ___uniting of opposites

___opposing forces   ___self-nurturance   ___happiness/celebration   ___integration

___competition/challenge   ___working/playing

Other: _____

Portrayed as: Reality __ __ __ __ __ Fantasy

10. COGNITIVE DEVELOPMENT AND SCENE PROGRESS

Cognition: ___age appropriate   Scene progress: ___continuous

          ___regressive to approx. age___   ___regressive (explain)

          ___advanced for age   ___progressive (explain)

                             ___resolution of conflict

                                 (restructuring of previous scene #___)

_____

_____

11. COORDINATION OF WHOLE AND PARTS OF THE SCENE

___chaotic or no coordination of figures or scene   ___empty

___partial attempts to coordinate   ___overemphasis of rows

___some coordination in small groupings   ___chaotic destruction of scene during process

___appears equally coordinated and chaotic   ___destruction of scene following completion

___mostly coordinated with minimum chaos

___scene coordinated as a whole

12. STRUCTURING OF RELATIONSHIPS (human and animal)

___no relationships represented   ___opposing groups and/or individuals   ___dyadic relationships

___a distinct separation of figure/s   ___individual/s relating to self or environment   ___family unit/s

                           ___one or more communities/groupings

Interactions portrayed between them:

___destructive/sadistic   ___self-protective/assertive   ___cooperative/constructive

13. BOUNDARIES

___entire scene runs together   ___some groupings with no clear boundaries

___boundary formation through:

        ___groupings ___use of space ___natural/man-made dividers ___containment ___dramatic play

___very fenced and/or rigid world   ___figures sit on or spill over sides of the tray

___figures and objects sink into the sand   ___boundaries invaded

14. MOVEMENT/OBSTACLES

___static scene with no sense of movement   ___destructive movement

___chaotic and undirected movement   ___movement with appropriate obstacles

___movement blocked (describe)   ___free-flow of movement with no obstacles

___parts of scene blocked, other parts not (describe)   ___movement inward toward the center

___some blockage, but movement can progress or go around (describe)

15. RELATIONSHIP OF PARTS AND OPPOSITES

Parts/opposites represented:_____

___opposites kept separate   ___no attempt to unify opposites   ___no opposites represented

___negative interaction of opposites   ___opposites unified

___positive interaction of opposites   ___opposites integrated

___attempt to unify opposites through: ___roads, rivers, etc.   ___bridges   ___figure placement

       ___dramatic play (describe) _____

16. THERAPIST'S IMPRESSION OF THE SCENE

___confusing/conflicting (exp.) ___self-destructive   ___angry/fearful/sad/painful ___peaceful, calm

___disruptive (explain)   ___no feeling or connection   ___colorful, happy   ___spiritual

___disconnected   ___lacking color, depressive   ___positive and moving

17. SIGNIFICANT SYMBOLIC REPRESENTATIONS AND THEMATIC PLAY

18. SIGNIFICANT REPETITIVE THEME AND FIGURES USED

19. QUESTIONS RAISED

NOTES

1 Geri Grubbs, *A categorical and comparative analysis of the sand play process of abused and nonabused children.* Unpublished doctoral dissertation. (California Graduate School of Family Psychology, San Rafael, CA, 1991).

2 Ruth Bowyer, *The Lowenfeld world technique* (London: Pergammon Press, 1970).

3 L. Jones, *The development of structure in the world of expression: A cognitive-developmental analysis of children's "sandworlds."* Unpublished doctoral dissertation. (Pacific Graduate School of Psychology, Palo Alto, CA, 1982).

4 Jeannette Pruyn Reed, *Sand magic: Experience in miniature - A nonverbal therapy for children* (New Mexico: privately published, 1975).

5 Dora Kalff, *Sandplay: A psychotherapeutic approach to the psyche* (Santa Monica, California, Sigo Press, 1980).

6 Yasunobu Okada, "Studies on the sand play technique: A study on the area of the sand play picture" in *Kyoto University Research Studies in Education,* vol. 18, 1972, pgs. 231-244.

7 Carl Jung, *The collected works of C. G. Jung,* H. Read, et.al, (Ed.) (Princeton: Bollingen Series XX, 1954).

8 Jean Piaget, *The psychology of the child* (New York: Basic Books, Inc., 1969).

9 Kay Bradway, *Sandplay bridges and the transcendent function* (San Francisco: C. G. Jung Institute, 1985).

BIBLIOGRAPHY and RESOURCES

Ammann, Ruth. *Healing and transformation in sandplay: Creative processes becoming visible.* La Salle, Illinois: Open Court, 1991.

Bowyer, Ruth. *The Lowenfeld world technique.* London: Pergammon Press, 1970.

Bradway, Kay. *Sandplay bridges and the transcendent function.* San Francisco: C. G. Jung Institute, 1985.

Bradway, Kay; McCoard, Barbara. *Sandplay: silent workshop of the psyche.* London: Routledge, 1997.

Cirlot, J. E. *A dictionary of symbols.* New York: Philosophical Library, 1962.

DeVries, Ad. *Dictionary of symbols and imagery.* Amsterdam: North-Holland Publishing Co, 1984.

Dundas, Evalyn. *Symbols come alive in the sand.* Boston: Coventure, Ltd, 1978.

Eastwood, Pratibha. *Nine Windows to Wholeness: exploring numbers in Sandplay therapy.* Hawaii: Sanity Press, 2002.

Friedman, Harriet; Mitchell, Rie Rogers. *Sandplay: past, present and future.* London: Routledge, 1994.

Grubbs, Geri. *A categorical and comparative analysis of the sandplay process of abused and nonabused children.* Doctoral dissertation: California Graduate School of Family Psychology, San Rafael, CA, 1991.

_____ "Into the wound: the psychic healing of abused children." In *Journal of Sandplay Therapy,* vol. IV, no. 1 (1994), 67-85.

_____ "A comparative analysis of the sandplay process of sexually abused and nonclinical children." In *The arts in psychotherapy*, vol. 22, no. 5 (1995), 429-446.

_____ "An abused child's use of sandplay in the healing process." In *Clinical Social Work Journal,* vol. 22, no. 2, (1994), 193-209.

Jones, L. *The development of structure in the world of expression: A cognitive-developmental analysis of children's "sandworlds."* Unpublished doctoral dissertation. Pacific Graduate School of Psychology, Palo Alto, CA, 1982.

Hill, G. (Ed.) *Sandplay studies: origins, theory, and practice.* San Francisco: C. G. Jung Institute, 1981.

Jung, Carl. *The collected works of C. G. Jung.* Read, H. et.al, (Ed.). Princeton: Bollingen Series XX. 1954.

Kalff, Dora. *Sandplay: A psychotherapeutic approach to the psyche.* Santa Monica, California: Sigo Press, 1980. Republished by Temenos Press, 2003.

Mitchell, Rie, and Friedman, Harriet. *Sandplay: past, present & future.* New York: Routledge, 1994.

Okada, Yasunobu. "Studies on the sand play technique: A study on the area of the sand play picture." In *Kyoto University Research Studies in Education,* vol. 18, 231-244, 1972.

Piaget, Jean. *The psychology of the child.* New York: Basic Books, Inc., 1969.

Reed, Jeannette. *Sand magic: Experience in miniature - A nonverbal therapy for children.* New Mexico: privately published, 1975.

Walker, Barbara. *The woman's dictionary of symbols and sacred objects.* San Francisco: Harper/San Francisco, 1988.

Weinrib, Estelle. *Images of the self.* Massachusetts: Sigo Press, 1983. Republished by Temenos Press, 2004.

About the Author and Researcher

Geri Grubbs, Ph.D., is a doctor of marriage, family and child therapy and certified Jungian Analyst on the board of the North Pacific Institute for Analytical Psychology. Her private practice is in Woodinville, Washington.

A graduate of the C. G. Jung Institute, Zurich, Switzerland, Dr. Grubbs also studied with sandplay founder, Dora Kalff. She is a teaching member of the International Society of Sandplay Therapists (ISST) and Sandplay Therapists of America (STA) that follows the teaching of Dora Kalff.

In addition to her research and publication of the Sandplay Categorical Checklist (SCC), she has published "**Bereavement Dreaming and the Individuating Soul,**" (Nicolas-Hays, Inc., 2004), a book on dreams had following the loss of a loved one.

Dr. Grubbs conducts sandplay workshops at her practice in Woodinville, and is available for consultation, supervision, and personal sandplay experience.

Visit her website at: www.EastsideJung.com

Made in the USA
Middletown, DE
23 November 2017